FLOWER DESIGN

Variations on the Basics

Also by June Kahl

Sketchbook of Easy Flower Designs

Sketchbook of Creativity

Flower Design Made Easy

JUNE ROBISON KAHL

FLOWER DESIGN

Variations on the Basics

Illustrations
  Ellen Oliver Parsons

Photographs
  Ken Hostetter

Prospect Hill Press
Baltimore

Dedication

To my grandchildren, Elizabeth Ann and Andrew George, with love.

Acknowledgments

With appreciation to editor and publisher Eleanor Heldrich for all her help and support throughout the writing of this book.

With untold thanks to artist Ellen Parsons for the beautiful cover design and the illustrations in the book.

To the photographer Ken Hostetter for all his time and the ability to produce the pictures that are such an important part of this book.

With appreciation to Annette Richter for the use of her pair of containers used in Design V.

Cover and interior art by Ellen Parsons.

Typeset and layout by Madeleine Adamson.

Printed in Hong Kong under the direction of Four Color Imports, Ltd.

Library of Congress Cataloging-in-Publication Data

Kahl, June Robison.
    Flower design : variations on the basics / June Robison Kahl ;
illustration, Ellen Oliver Parsons ; photographs, Ken Hostetter.
        p.   cm.
    Includes index.
    ISBN 0-941526-09-7
    1. Flower arrangement.   I. Title.
SB449.K23 1994   94-29055
745.92--dc20   CIP

Published by

Prospect Hill Press
216 Wendover Road
Baltimore, MD 21218-1837
(410) 889-0320

Table of Contents

Introduction

Welcome to the wonderful world of flower design! Knowing a few basic designs and having the confidence to apply your knowledge and skills in flower arranging to suit the time, place, color, and space available will give you many hours of pleasure and you will gain well-deserved pride in your accomplishments.

This book was written to help you reach these goals. Easy to follow instructions with photographs and diagrams show how to make each design. To add interest, basic designs have been combined to create new designs. These variations are meant to intrigue and stimulate your imagination so that your own beautiful designs will result.

By following the instructions in this book, first the basic designs and then the new interpretations, your confidence will begin to grow and the completed arrangements will please you and add beauty to your home. Ideally, you can grow flowers, design floral arrangements, and enjoy their beauty inside as well as out-of-doors.

Fundamentals of Flower Design

Containers are an important part of any design. They may be plain, elaborate, or abstract, depending on the desired effect of the completed design. Determining the color of a container depends on many factors. What color goes with the decor of the home? What color is best for a flower show? What color will complement the flowers to be used? All of these factors are important to consider.

Pinholders come in many sizes and shapes. The size pinholder to use depends on the size of the arrangement desired and the size of the container. Never use a pinholder that is larger than needed because a pinholder is a mechanical device that should not be seen. Pincups are useful when a large amount of water is not required and in abstract designs where a traditional container is not used. All fresh plant material requires water.

Plan your garden so you have an available supply of plant material. Trees and shrubs should be selected with their foliage and flowers in mind. Plant bulbs and grow flowers that are the color you like to use in flower designs. Think about the growing season in your area and plant accordingly. Try to plan so that something is blooming the entire growing season. Florist flowers are costly, especially when doing a mass design which requires many flowers, but there are designs in the book which use just a few flowers or dried plant material.

Begin keeping a notebook of designs. Sketch designs before you actually make them. This way you will know how many flowers will be needed before going to the florist. Your notebook will become a good reference book. Ideas come from many sources, not just from your own imagination. When attending a flower design program, sketch some of the speaker's designs; or if visiting a museum, be prepared to sketch anything that may suggest a flower design.

Flower design has an interesting history. There are Oriental, European, and American designs. Oriental designs are linear and require few flowers, while European designs are often masses which require many flowers. American designs are a combination of both.

Certain procedures must be followed for every flower design. Select fresh flowers that are not fully open. Condition them by cutting off the bottom of each stem and standing them in a tall container of tepid water for several hours or overnight. And finally, before placing any flower in a design, strip off all the leaves that will be under water, as they will decay and foul the water.

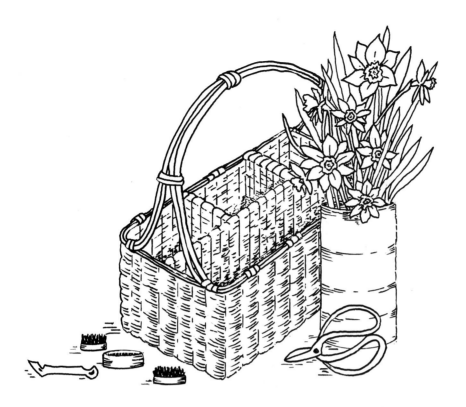

Flower Arranger's Workbasket

A flower arranger is an artist working with live plant material; and, like any artist, will need some basic tools and equipment. Keeping everything together in one place, ready to use, is the function of an arranger's workbasket. It should include:

1. Flower scissors with sharp, straight blades to cut stems so they can absorb water easily.

2. Pinholders and pincups, to hold flowers.

3. Floral clay, to attach pinholders to containers.

4. Oasis or green plastic floral foam to hold flowers in container when pinholders cannot be used.

5. Can opener, to remove pinholders from containers.

6. Floral wire (straight) of medium gauge (#20), to hold plant material in place.

7. Tall container for water to condition flowers.

To Prepare Plant Material

1. Flowers should be fresh and at the height of their perfection.

2. Condition all flowers immediately by cutting off at least one inch of stem, preferably under water. Strip off bottom leaves and place in a deep container of tepid water. Leave in water several hours or overnight to harden before arranging. Exception: daffodils require shallow water.

3. Wash all foliage to remove dust. Remove broken or damaged leaves.

4. Start with a clean container and pinholder. Only use new Oasis.

5. Sit with container directly in front of you.

6. Attach pinholder to dry container.

7. Fill container with water before you start to make a design.

8. Remember that the first placement is the most important. Select the most beautiful and the strongest of the plant material for the #1 placement in each design.

9. Supplies may be purchased from florist or garden center.

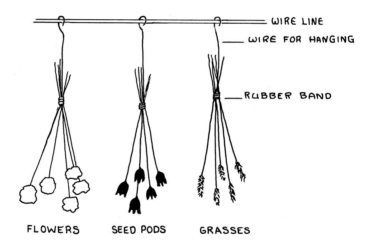

To Dry Plant Material

1. Air Drying. Strip the leaves from the stems of flowers. Bind them together with rubber bands, and hang by bunches upside down in a cool, dry, dark place. Easy plant materials to dry are hardy annuals, grasses, seed pods. Make sure that air is able to circulate around the flower heads. Wire each bunch to a plastic-coated wire coat hanger.

2. Glycerine. Mix one part glycerine to two parts hot water. Crush or split the ends of branches and immerse them in 3" or 4" of the solution until the leaves change color. This is the best method for preserving leaves such as beech or aspidistra.

3. Drying In Water. This method may be used for plants with exceptionally strong stems, such as yarrow, hydrangea, and many grasses. Pick the flowers at the height of their beauty just before they begin to dry on the plant and keep them in a container of water until they dry.

FLORAL CLAY — PINHOLDER

To Attach A Pinholder

1. To attach a pinholder to a container, both container and pinholder must be dry. First roll a piece of floral clay, between both hands, into a long, slender cigarette shape.

2. Attach this roll of clay to the outer edge of an upside down pinholder, making sure you join the two ends together.

3. Place the pinholder in the container and press down hard, giving it a slight twist. This will create suction that holds the pinholder in place.

4. Fill container with water before starting the design.

STEM —

WIRE HERE →
STEM —

To Bend Fresh Plant Material

1. Start halfway up the stem.

2. Place both thumbs touching underneath stem with other fingers over top of stem.

3. Gently apply pressure where the bend is to start. Continue to the end of the branch.

4. Keep applying pressure while moving fingers to end of the branch or flower.

5. Repeat this procedure until the stem is bent as much as desired.

6. To make a loop, bring tip around until it crosses main stem. Cut a 1 1/2" piece of medium-gauge florist wire. Bend the piece of wire around the main stem and tip of the plant material. The turns of the wire should be as neat and close together as possible. Do not twist wire. Simply bend it around the stems.

The Basic Designs

The first six flower arrangements in the book are the basic designs on which the interpretations in this book are based. Different flowers and foliage may be substituted for those suggested here. Remember, the larger the design, the more flowers and foliage that will be required. Practice making these basic designs until you are able to do them quickly and easily. New interpretation in flower designing usually means combining two or more basic designs to form one new design.

Containers for basic designs are very plain and of simple design with colors that are neutral or muted.

Vertical Design

Container

Green round pedestal

Plant Material

5 purple liatris

5 yucca leaves

Mechanics

Pinholder

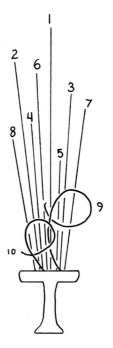

Placement on Pinholder

Procedure

Cut and place on the pinholder in the following order.

#1, #2 and #3 liatris approximately 16", 14" and 12".

#4 and #5 liatris approximately 10" and 7".

#6, #7 and #8 yucca leaves 13", 11" and 9".

#9 and #10 yucca leaves are the tallest available. Bend each into a circle and fasten with a straight pin.

Substitute Plant Material

1. Blue iris and iris foliage.

2. Tulips and pussy willow.

Mass Design

Container

Low pink marble pedestal

Plant Material

9 purple liatris

5 pink mini-carnations sprays

5 stems of Baker fern

Mechanics

Pinholder

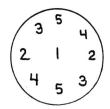

Placement on Pinholder

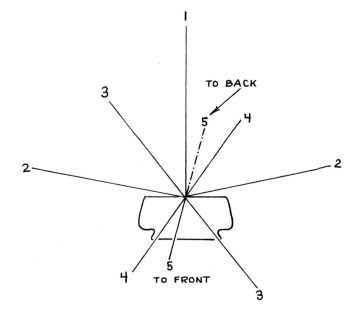

Procedure

Cut #1 liatris 14" and place in the center of the pinholder.

#2's each 12" and place low to each side.

#3's each 10" and place slightly higher than #2's, one to the front and one to the back.

#4's each 8" and place higher than #3's, one to the front and one to the back.

#5's each 5" and place in front and in back of #1.

Cut each mini-spray carnation a different length and place between the liatris.

Place filler green, the Baker fern, under #1 and throughout the design going in the same direction as, and always shorter than, the flowers.

Substitute Plant Material

1. Nine snapdragons, six carnations, two mini-carnation sprays.

2. Nine zinnias, eight small marigolds.

Asymmetrical Design

Container

    Low, round, brown container

Plant Material

    5 pink snapdragons

    5 pink carnations

Mechanics

    Pinholder

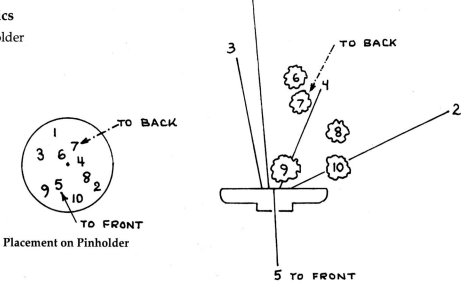

Placement on Pinholder

Procedure

    Cut and place on the pinholder in the following order:

        #1, #2, #3, #4 and #5 snapdragons approximately 14", 11", 9", 7" and 5".

        #6, #7, #8, #9 and #10 carnations approximately 8", 7", 6", 5" and 4".

    Cut filler plant material, such as Baker fern, different lengths and place in and around the carnations.

Note: An asymmetrical design is one half of a mass.

Substitute Plant Material

    1. Liatris and tulips.

    2. Cattails and chrysanthemums.

Horizontal Design

Container

Narrow dark-blue oval

Plant Material

6 branches of plum-yew
(cephalotaxus)

6 red carnations

Mechanics

Pinholder

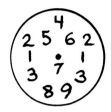

Placement on Pinholder

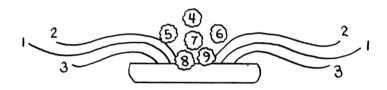

Procedure

Attach pinholder in center of container.

Place the longest plum-yew branches, the #1's, to right and left sides. Bend branches if necessary for a graceful line. See page 11.

Cut #2's shorter than #1's. Place slightly higher than #1's.

#3's shorter than #2's. Place lower than #1's.

Cut #4 carnation slightly higher than #2 branches. Place in the center back.

#5 and #6 slightly shorter than #4. Place to the left and right of #4.

#7 slightly shorter than #5 and #6. Place in front of #4.

#8 and #9 shorter than #7. Place to right and left of #7.

Add three small sprays of leaves behind the carnations, one to the left, one in the middle and one to the right.

Substitute Plant Material

1. Flowering crab apple branches and five daffodils.

2. Holly branches and five red carnations.

3. Dried wheat and three to five dahlias, depending on size.

Diagonal Design

Container

Pewter chalice

Plant Material

6 branches pussy willow

3 orange lily sprays

Mechanics

Oasis, cut to fit

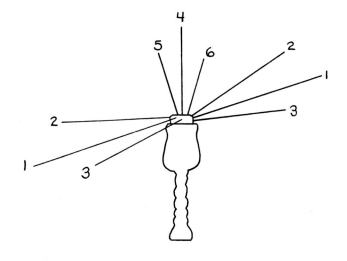

Procedure

Cut Oasis to fit container, extending an inch above the rim.

Cut #1's the longest pussy willows and place into the Oasis above the rim to the left and right, slanting in opposite directions.

#2's shorter than #1's and place to the left and right above the #1's.

#3's shorter than #2's and place to the left and right below the #1's.

Cut #4 lily spray so that it is slightly higher than the pussy willows and place in the center of the container.

#5 slightly shorter than #4 and place to the left of #4.

#6 slightly shorter than #5 and place to the right of #4.

Arrange some filler foliage around the lily sprays.

Filler Foliage

Fern, acuba, or lemon leaves.

Substitute Flowers

1. Tulips and tulip foliage.

2. Roses and rose leaves.

3. Peonies and peony leaves.

Line Design

Container

    Black plastic oval

Plant Material

    3 branches Magnolia soulangeana

    2 red ginger flowers

Mechanics

    Pinholder

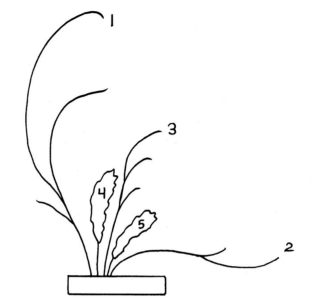

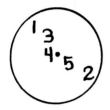

Placement on Pinholder

Procedure

    Attach pinholder in the left back of the container.

    All branches should be facing into the center of the design. Bend branches if necessary for a graceful line. See page 11.

    Place #1 tallest branch in the left back.

        #2 low and in the right front.

        #3 slightly forward and to the right of #1.

    Cut #4 flower short and place in front of #3, leaning slightly forward.

        #5 shorter than #4 and place to the right of #4, leaning forward.

    Place two ginger leaves, one to the left and one to the right of the flowers.

Substitute Flowers and Branches

    1. Forsythia branches and five daffodils.

    2. Crab apple branches and three tulips.

    3. Any flowering branch and two or three flowers, depending on size.

    4. Holly branches and one poinsettia.

The Variations

Before creating a new look in flower design one must understand and be able to execute the basic designs. It is important to know how to arrange flowers and foliage in an orderly manner and how to cut and condition plant material. This makes one aware of the structures and shapes of fresh plant material. It is this awareness that leads to creativity and new interpretations.

There are two ways to approach creating a new look. The first method is to look very closely at plant materials and then decide which basic design is best suited for that particular flower or branch. The second approach is to start with an idea for a design and then select the plant material that would be best for that purpose.

New interpretations are accomplished by combining two or more basic designs into a single new design. For example, combine a vertical design with a diagonal design. This book has many suggestions for combining different designs. The instructions start with the preparations required and then continue with the step-by-step procedures for placing the plant material in the proper places. *Flower Design, Variations on the Basics* is a review of the basics with emphasis on new interpretations.

Design I: Creative Vertical

CREATIVE VERTICAL: The dominant thrust of the design must be vertical. There may be more than one point of emergence and more than one focal area if it does not destroy the vertical thrust.

Container

Tall bamboo pottery

Plant Material

6 equisetum (horsetail)

6 yucca leaves

2 sprays of yellow lilies

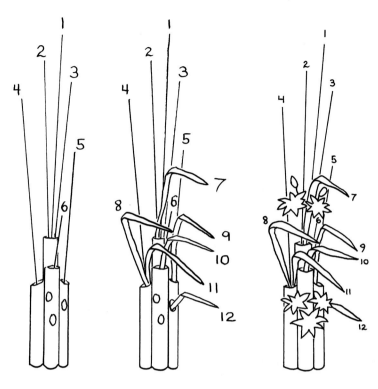

Procedure

Equisetum is the tallest plant material. Cut different lengths to vary their heights.

Place #1 equisetum, the tallest, in center back.

> #2 and #3, the next tallest, on each side of #1.

> #4 to the left of #2.

> #5 to the right of #3.

> #6 in front of and in between #3 and #5.

Yucca leaves are cut as long as possible. Place them in the container before bending. Vary the height of each leaf by varying the place where each is bent. All should be bent toward the right.

Place #7, the tallest yucca, in front of #3 in right center.

> #8, the next tallest, to the far right in front of #4.

> #9 in front of #5.

> #10 in front of #6.

> #11 to left in front of #2.

> #12 low and in the center front.

Cut the first spray of lilies long enough to be placed in front of #1 and #2 equisetum and under #7 yucca.

Place the second lily spray low and in the center front.

Substitute Container for Design I

Use a small low container and place a large round pinholder in the center; or make your own natural bamboo container.

Placement on Pinholder

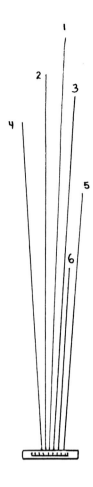

To Make A Natural Bamboo Container

Saw a bamboo pole that is 1" in diameter into various lengths.

Make the first cut on an angle and the second cut straight.

Always saw between the solid knots in the bamboo. Make six or seven cuts.

To assemble: using a large round pinholder, mount the bamboo on the pinholder, placing the tallest piece to the back and working toward the front. A hammer and chisel may be needed as the dried bamboo is very hard.

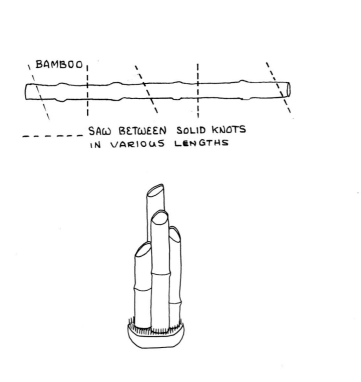

SAW BETWEEN SOLID KNOTS
IN VARIOUS LENGTHS

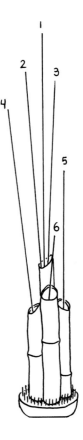

Substitute Plant Materials For A Holiday Design

1. Straight pieces of holly and poinsettia flowers.

    To Condition Poinsettia Flowers:

    Cut poinsettia flower to desired length.

    Sear the cut end using a candle.

    Also sear any place where leaves have been removed.

    Immediately place in tepid water and leave overnight before placing in a design.

    Flowers are long-lasting if properly conditioned.

2. Magnolia leaves and artichoke flowers.

To Make Artichoke Flowers

Buy four different size artichokes. Place on top of small juice glasses until they become soft and begin to change color. Green artichokes are brittle and hard to open. Usually it takes three or four days before they can be opened easily.

Cut in half a number of round wooden toothpicks. These will be used to hold open the leaves.

For all four artichokes:

1. Pull off the very small leaves at the top of the stem. Cut the length of the stem to one inch.

2. Pierce the stem, as close as possible, under the leaves with a thin nail or skewer and insert a round wooden toothpick.

3. Place artichoke in palm of the left hand with the stem between fingers.

4. Using both thumbs, gently open artichoke—starting at the outside edge and working toward the center.

STOP at this point for a bud.

CONTINUE for a half-open bud.

5. Starting with the outer row of leaves, open each leaf as far as possible and insert a half-toothpick at the base of the leaf to keep it open.

6. Work around the artichoke in this manner for three or four rows.

STOP at this point for a half-open bud.

CONTINUE for a half-open rose.

7. For the next three rows, cut off the tips of each of the remaining leaves. Bend each leaf in toward the center. Always work from outside edge toward the center. Be careful not to break or crease the leaf while bending. Place a half-toothpick at the base of each bent leaf to hold it in place.

STOP at this point for a half-open rose.

CONTINUE for a full rose.

8. Begin with steps 1 through 4.

9. Bend all leaves in toward the center. Insert a half-toothpick at the base of each leaf to keep it open.

Artichoke flowers (left to right): half-open bud, half-open rose, full rose.

10. Cut off the remaining small leaves in the center of the artichoke to make a flat center.

Stop at this point for a full rose.

Continue for ALL artichoke flowers.

11. Place the artichokes on top of small juice glasses to dry.

12. Check occasionally to make sure all leaves are in the correct position. If not, re-insert a half-toothpick to hold them in place. It takes several weeks for them to dry. When dry, they are very light in weight.

13. Remove all the toothpicks, including the one in the stem.

14. Place a 12" length of wire in the hole in the stem and bend in half. This wire is then attached to a branch and the artichoke flower is ready to be placed in a flower design.

Note: Other ways to use artichoke flowers:

1. In holiday designs, spray them with gold.

2. In dried designs, use them in natural color.

3. To use in Christmas wreaths, attach to a grapevine wreath. Insert fresh foliage around the artichoke flowers. Add a colorful bow.

Design II: Creative Vertical

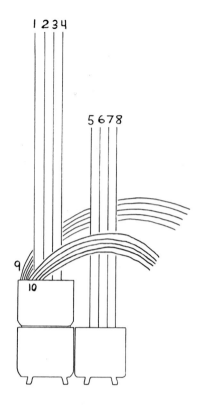

Containers

3 red pottery squares

Plant material

8 purple liatris

1 bunch of bear grass

Mechanics

2 square pinholders
approximately 3"

or 2 rectangular pinholders

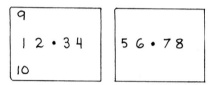

Placement on Pinholders

Preparation

Place one container on top of another one.

Place the third container against the stacked ones.

Attach the pinholders in center of containers.

Procedure

Cut 4 liatris all the same height and place in a horizontal line across the center of the tallest container.

Cut remaining 4 liatris shorter than the liatris in the tall container. Place in a horizontal line across the center of the low container.

All flowers should be in a straight line in the containers. Cut off the tips of all the flowers so they are absolutely even at the top.

Divide the bear grass in half and place a rubber band around the bottom of each group of stems. Cut off stems evenly.

Bend each bunch over from top toward the bottom and hold until it falls into a graceful curve. See page 11. Do not remove rubber band.

Place one half in the left back corner of the tall container, behind the liatris, and falling toward the right.

Place the second bunch in the left front corner of the tall container so that it falls in front of the liatris.

The liatris in the low container will be between the two curving branches of bear grass.

Trim the curving bear grass so that none of the tips touch the table.

Substitute Containers: Any tall and low container combination.

Substitute Plant Material: For the liatris, any spike flower such as gladioli or snapdragon. For the bear grass, any cascading flower such as sweet pea, wisteria, or lilac.

Design III: Horizontal Design

HORIZONTAL DESIGN: is always wider than it is tall. The center should be slightly raised, not overly compact, and tapering to the sides. It is usually symmetrical. Creative horizontal designs are usually asymmetrical.

Container

Black cylinder

Plant Material

7 branches of Spirea vanhouttei

3 sprays of peach lilies

Mechanics

None, because the branches support the flowers

ASYMMETRICAL

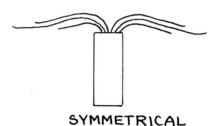

SYMMETRICAL

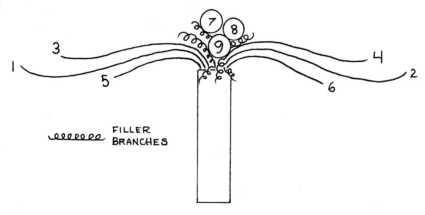

Proce

Select two long, graceful, same-length spirea branches and bend the stems to fit into the container.

Place #1 to the left and #2 to the right.

Cut #3 and #4 shorter than #1 and #2. Place in back of #1 and #2.

Cut #5 and #6 shorter than #3 and #4. Place in front of #1 and #2.

Cut lily spray #7 to be slightly higher than #3 and #4 spirea. Place to the back of the container.

Cut lilies #8 and #9 slightly shorter than #7. Place to the front of #7.

Filler branch: Cut the remaining spirea branch into three or four short pieces. Place where needed to fill in under and around the lily sprays.

Comment: This design looks very graceful in a tall container. However, it can be made in a low narrow container which is appropriate for placing on a mantel or on a speaker's table.

Design IV: Vertical and Horizontal Combination

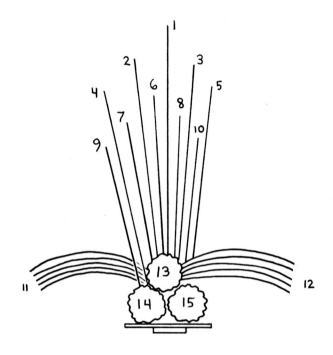

Container

Low black plastic from florist

Plant Material

10 liatris

3 hot pink gerberas

1 bunch of bear grass

Mechanics

1 large pinholder

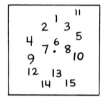

Placement on Pinholder

Always exaggerate the height of the vertical when combining a vertical with a horizontal design.

Preparation

Attach pinholder in center of the container.

Divide the bear grass in half. Place a small rubber band about one inch from the bottom of each bunch. Cut off the bottoms of the stems so they are even.

Bend each bunch of bear grass into a graceful curve. See page 11. Do not remove rubber bands.

Procedure

The liatris flowers are placed in a fan pattern, across the back part of the pinholder. The stems are placed next to one another and then slightly slanted apart at the top.

Liatris

Cut #1 twenty-six inches long. Place in center back.

#2 and #3 two inches shorter. Place to the left and right of #1.

#4 and #5 one inch shorter. Place to the left of #2 and the right of #3.

#6 eighteen inches long. Place in front of #1.

#7 and #8 two inches shorter than #6. Place in front of #2 and #3.

#9 and #10 one inch shorter. Place in front of #4 and #5.

Bear Grass

Place #11 in back of #5 and falling to the left.

#12 in front of #9 and falling to the right.

Cut off any bear grass ends that are touching the table.

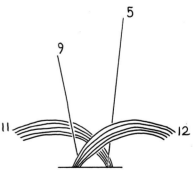

Placement of Bear Grass

Gerberas

The three gerberas are placed in a triangle in the center of the design, in front of #6, #7 and #8.

Cut #13 about five inches long. Place in front of #6.

#14 and #15 shorter than #13. Place in front of #7 and #8.

Note: An interesting variation is to cut all the gerberas the same length and place in a straight line across the bottom of the design. Placements are the same—in front of #6, #7 and #8.

Design V: Diagonal and Vertical Combination

Containers

    1 black

    1 white

Plant Material

    9 pussy willow branches

    5 hot pink gerberas

Mechanics

    2 pinholders

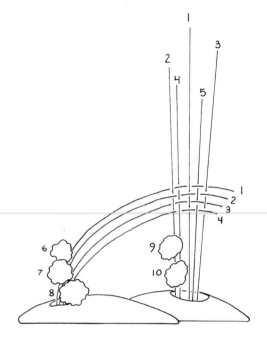

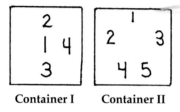

Container I   Container II

Preparation

    Attach one pinholder on the left side of Container I.

    Attach second pinholder on right side of Container II.

Procedure for Container I Diagonal

    Hold 4 pieces of pussy willow in left hand. Arrange so that each one is 1" to 1 1/2" shorter than the preceding one. Cut off, evenly, the bottom of the stems.

    Gently bend each one so it forms a graceful curve. See page 11. All four lean to the right.

    Place #1 pussy willow, the tallest, in center of pinholder.

        #2 to the right back of #1.

        #3 to the right front of #1.

        #4 to the right of #2 and #3 and opposite #1.

Procedure for Container II Vertical

    Hold 5 straight pieces of pussy willow in left hand. Arrange so that each one is 1" to 1 1/2" shorter than the preceding one. Cut off, evenly, the bottom of the stems.

    Place #1 pussy willow, the tallest, in the center back of the pinholder.

        #2 to the left of #1 and slightly forward.

        #3 to the right of #1 and slightly forward.

        #4 between #1 and #2 and slightly forward.

        #5 slightly forward and to right of #4.

To Assemble The Design

Place Container I to the left side and Container II to the right back of Container I. The left end of Container II should touch the right end of Container I.

Weave the diagonal branches of pussy willow through the vertical branches. Place some to the back, some to the middle and some to the front of the vertical branches.

Container I Flowers:

Place #6 and #7 flowers on the left side of the pussy willow branches.

#8 low and in front of the pussy willow.

Container II Flowers

Place #9 flower on the left side of the pussy willow.

#10 under #9 and in front of the pussy willow.

Substitute Plant Material: For a Spring design, daffodils or tulips with pussy willow.

Substitute Container: One large low container may be used for this design. Place one large pinholder to the extreme left and one to the extreme right in the container. Use only three diagonal and four vertical branches and three flowers in the design.

Design VI: Parallel

PARALLEL: a design with three or more vertical groupings of materials. Negative spaces between the groupings are important. Plant materials are positioned in a strong vertical manner. Units may be of one plant material, a combination of materials, or the same plant materials repeated in each unit.

Container

2 similar white ones, touching each other

Plant Material

8 forsythia branches

6 okra pods

6 white larkspur

Mechanics

None

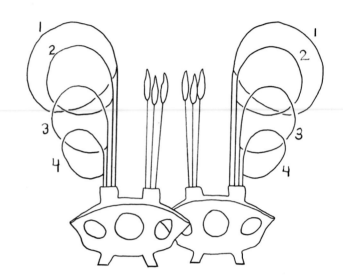

Preparation

Cut eight straight forsythia branches and strip off all leaves and small side branches.

Bend into various size circles. Wire at the places where the branches cross, using 1" of wire to wrap around the stems. See page 11. Allow to dry for several weeks.

Paint the forsythia circles and the okra pods white.

Place the two containers end to end touching each other to form one container.

Procedure

Place four circles of varying sizes in each end of the containers.

Start with the largest at the top and work toward the smallest at the bottom. Four face to the left, and four to the right.

Place three okra pods in each of the center openings.

Cut the larkspur short and fill in the center of each of the okra clusters. **Remember** to keep the spaces open between the vertical groups.

Substitute Flowers: For larkspur and okra, delphinium or gladioli.

Substitute Container: One long narrow container with four pinholders or four small containers, all alike, placed end to end.

Note: For a more dramatic effect, paint the branches the same color as the flowers; however, they are not required to be the same color.

Design VII: Traditional Mass Design

MASS DESIGN: is characterized by the use of a large quantity of plant material; the plant material is never crowded, but the design has a closed silhouette.

Preparation

Cut Oasis to fit the container, then cut off a one-inch slice from each corner, top to bottom. This makes it easier to place flowers on the corners. Never fill a container completely with Oasis. Leave room around the Oasis for water.

Attach pinholder to center of container. See page 11. Next push a small square of nylon down over the pinpoints. Then push down the Oasis. Later, just pull up on the ends of the nylon square to pull the Oasis from the pinholder.

Container

8" Oriental bowl with base

Plant Material

9 yellow snapdragons

10 blue delphiniums

12 yellow carnations

5 sprays of peach lilies

5 sprays of yellow spider
    chrysanthemums

1 bunch white montecasino

Mechanics

1 large pinholder

2/3 block of Oasis

6" square of stocking nylon

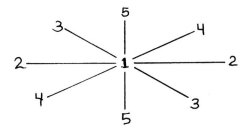

LOOKING DOWN ON DESIGN

Procedure

Both sides of the design are similar.

The #1 flower is the tallest with the best flower.

Step 1 - Snapdragons

Cut #1 to the desired height. Place in center of pinholder.

#2's slightly shorter than #1. Place low and to each side leaning over container.

#3 flowers slightly shorter than #2's, one to the front and one to the back. Place slightly higher.

#4 flowers slightly longer than #3's. Place slightly higher, one to the front and one to the back.

#5 flowers so some of each flower is over the edge of the container. Place one in front and one in back of #1.

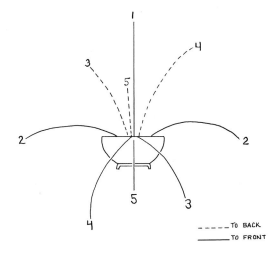

Step 2 - Delphiniums

Cut each flower shorter than each snapdragon.

Place between the snapdragons.

Cut several flowers very short.

Place them in the center of the design around #1.

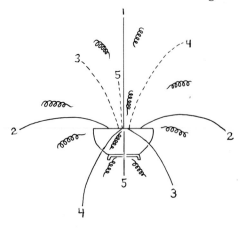

ᶜᶜᶜᶜᶜ— DELPHINIUMS

Step 3 - Carnations

Cut carnations various lengths, always shorter than snapdragons and delphiniums.

Place where needed at various locations in design.

Remember to cut some short and place in toward center of design.

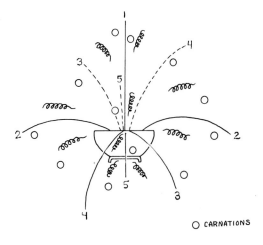

○ CARNATIONS

Step 4 - Lilies

The sprays of lilies are placed toward the center of the design near the #1 snapdragon.

Place the first lily to the center toward the top.

the second lower and toward center right.

the third low and to the left side.

Place the fourth and fifth lilies in the same location as second and third, however, on the other side of the design.

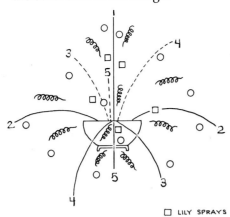

□ LILY SPRAYS

Step 5 - Chrysanthemums

Separate the sprays. Place the flowers where needed to fill a void.

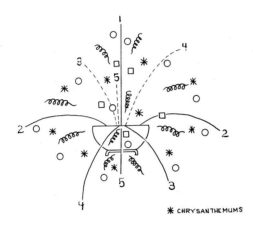

✻ CHRYSANTHEMUMS

Step 6 - Montecasino, white filler flowers.

Separate the sprays and place flowers where needed to fill a void.

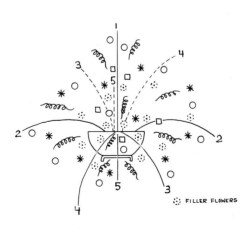

⋰ FILLER FLOWERS

Comment: Mass flower designs require a large amount of plant material and are expensive. Each design should have a minimum of three different varieties of flowers plus some filler flowers and foliage. Color coordination is very important. There should be a blending of colors plus a contrasting color. Equally important is the use of different forms of flowers and the gradation of their sizes.

Design VIII: Creative Triangle Mass

CREATIVE MASS DESIGN: a creative design which uses more plant material than other present day designs. There may be enclosed spaces resulting from the placement of line materials and these spaces are considered part of the mass. Groupings of plant materials of like colors, textures, and forms are massed along lines, or spaces made by lines. Containers are usually non-traditional. There may be more than one focal area and more than one point of emergence; however, the design is NOT abstract.

Container

Low purple oval

Plant Material

9 cattails
10-12 branches of artemisia

Mechanics

1 large round pinholder
or
2 large rectangular
   pinholders

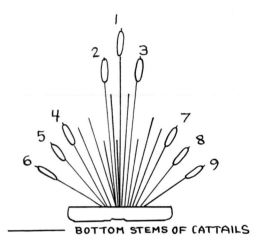

BOTTOM STEMS OF CATTAILS

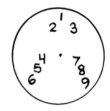

Placement on Pinholder

Preparation

To dry cattails, cut with long stems. Pour over each cattail head a mixture of one half shellac and one half denatured alcohol. Then place them upright in a carton of empty soft drink bottles. DO NOT let heads touch each other. Store in a dry, cool place for three to four weeks.

To dry artemisia, cut with long stems and hang them upside down in a dry place.

Procedure

Attach large pinholder in the center of container. See page 11.

Place #1 cattail (tallest) in center back of pinholder.

Cut #2 and #3 slightly shorter than #1. Place slightly forward on each side of #1.

#4 shorter than #2. Place on left side below #2. The space betwen #2 and #4 is greater than the space between #1 and #2.

#5 slightly longer than #4. Place on left below #4.

#6 slightly longer than #5. Place on left below #5, coming forward.

#7, #8 and #9 the same as #4, #5 and #6. Place on right below #3.

Cut the stems of the artemisia different lengths. Place the taller artemisia in the back and work forward. Place it around the cattail stems, some in back as well as in front. Keep the artemisia low enough to show off the stems of the cattails.

Make use of the stems that were cut from the nine cattails. Cut two as long as possible and place on each side of #1. Cut four and place two between #2 and #4 and two between #3 and #7. Cut the remaining three the same length and place them throughout the middle of the artemisia. All should lean forward in the design.

Comment: In a mass design, both sides are alike. The three groups of cattails form two sides of a triangle and the container and the low artemisia form the other side.

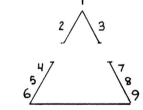

Substitute Container: A large, low container of any shape may be used.

Substitute Dried Plant Materials:

1. Teasels and cornflowers.

2. Okra and yarrow.

Substitute Fresh Plant Materials:

1. Gladioli and heather.

2. Delphinium and baby's breath.

3. Liatris and spray carnations.

Design IX: Creative Mass of All Dried Plant Material

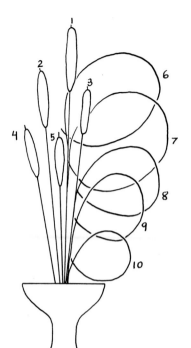

Container

Beige pedestal

Plant Material

5 cattails

5 forsythia branches

1 bunch of foxtail grass

Mechanics

Pinholder

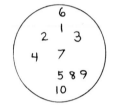

Placement on Pinholder

Preparation

Dry forsythia circles according to directions on page 42.

Dry cattails according to directions on page 48.

Arrange the cattails on a table with all the heads in a straight line and the uneven ends·of the stems over the edge.

Vary the height of the cattails by pulling each stem over the edge of the table so each is a different height. Vary the differences in the heights. Cut off stems in a straight line at the edge of the table.

Procedure

Place #1, the tallest cattail in the center back,

> #2 to the left and slightly forward of #1.

> #3 to the right and opposite to #2.

> #4 to the left and slightly forward of #2.

> #5 to the center between #4 and #3 and in center front of #1.

Arrange forsythia circles #6, #7, #8, #9, #10 on the table according to size, from the largest to the smallest. Cut off the stems so that the largest circle is the tallest and the smallest is the shortest.

Place #6 circle in back of #1.

> #7 in back of #5.

> #8 next to #5.

#9 next to #8.

#10 in front of #5 and leaning forward over right front of container.

Foxtail grass is a weed growing along the roadside. In the fall it dries to a lovely shade of
beige. Cut a large bunch and place a rubber band around the bottom of the stems and
hang to dry. When ready to use in a design, hold the foxtail grass, in the left hand, just
under the heads and place a rubber band on the ends of the stems about 1" from the
bottom. Cut off stems evenly. Cut short enough so some of the grass will fall grace-
fully over the edge of the container when it is placed in the center front of the design.
Do not remove rubber band.

Design X : Creative Mass of All Fresh Plant Material

Container

Tall pottery with two openings

Plant Material

3 lengths of bittersweet,
3 to 4 feet long

6 yucca leaves

Mechanics

None

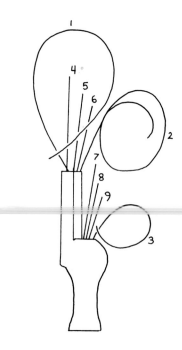

Preparation

Bend the bittersweet into three different size circles. The largest should have the longest stem while the smallest has the shortest stem.

Hold a stem in the left hand. Take the tip in the right hand and loop the bittersweet over to the left hand. Wire at the point where the two meet, using a 1" length of wire. Do not twist the wire, merely turn it around the stem several times. It should be neatly done. The wire does not have to be removed.

Note: For a stronger and heavier look, longer bittersweet vine may be looped several times before wiring.

Procedure

Bittersweet circles:

All circles should face the same way.

Place #1 in the top opening leaning to the left.

#2 in the top opening leaning to the right.

#3 (smallest circle) in the bottom opening, low and coming forward over the front of the container.

Yucca leaves:

Place #4, #5 and #6 leaves in the top opening with the tallest to the left.

#7, #8 and #9 in the bottom opening with the tallest leaf next to the side of the container.

Substitute Plant Material: Any vine, such as grape, honeysuckle, or wisteria without flowers, can be made into circles. If wisteria is in bloom, place the flower clusters so they hang downward over the container.

Substitute Container: Any pedestal container with a pinholder can be used.

Design XI: Creative Design In A Geometric Container Using Fresh And Dried Plant Material

CREATIVE DESIGNS: are eclectic in concept because they borrow from different styles and/ or periods, combining these features into new concepts and forms in flower design. A creative design is the result of a creative idea of the artist using plant material and other components to organize the elements, within the limits of the principles of design, to create an art form.

Container

Black ceramic triangle

Plant Material

3 forsythia branches
3 sprays of peach lilies,
   one with a bud

Mechanics

Pinholder

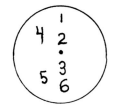

Placement on Pinholder

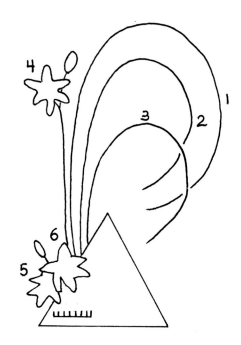

Preparation

Bend the forsythia branches into circles, see page 42. Allow them to dry. Paint, when dry, with glossy black paint.

Attach pinholder on left side of container. See page 11.

Procedure

Remove the wire from the dried forsythia branches so the circles open.

Place #1 circle, the largest, in middle back of pinholder.

   #2 circle, middle size, next to #1, coming forward in a straight line on the pinholder.

   #3 circle, smallest, next to #2 coming forward and in a straight line on the pinholder.

Cut off the open ends of the circles so they do not touch the container.

Place #4 lily spray with a bud on the left side of the branches and almost as high as #1.

   #5 lily low and to the left of #3.

   #6 slightly higher than #5 and in front of #3.

Substitute Container: Any low or compote-style container.

An Alternative Design With Fresh, Dried And Man-Made Materials

Container

Black ceramic triangle

Plant Material

3 red anthuriums

a strelitzia leaf

Manmade Material

3 feet of black wire

Balsa wood stick,
1/4" by 1/4" by 6"

Mechanics

2 pinholders

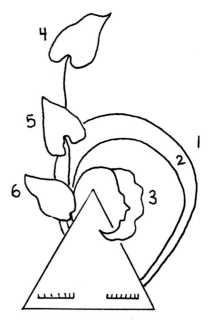

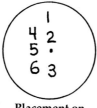

**Placement on
Left Pinholder**

**Placement on
Right Pinholder**

Preparation

Place one strelitzia leaf in a container of water until it dries. Drying in water is slower than air-drying; however, it keeps the leaf from closing up entirely. After it is dry, paint the leaf black.

Make two circles of different sizes using black wire that is stiff enough to hold its shape.

Cut four pieces of balsa wood, each 1 1/2" long.

Wire one piece of balsa wood to each end of the black wires, leaving a 1/4" piece of the wood extending beyond the wire.

Attach one pinholder to the left side of the container and one to the right side.

Procedure

Place one end of #1 wire circle to the back of the left pinholder and the other end to the back of the right pinholder. The balsa wood goes on the pinholder.

Place #2 wire circle in front of #1, one end to the left and one to the right.

> #3 leaf on the left side in front of #2 wire and leaning to the right over the edge of the container and lower than #1 and #2.

> #4, #5, and #6 anthuriums in a vertical line on the left side of the circles with the #4 flower higher than the circles. The #5 and #6 flowers are lower, looking up at the #4 flower.

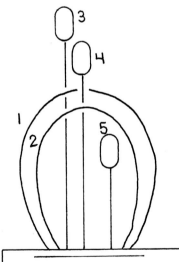

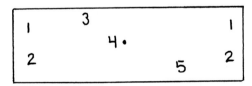

Placement on Pinholder

Note For A Design Without A Leaf

Use a low container and place one pinholder in the center. Begin by placing wire circles #1 and #2 on opposite sides of the pinholder. Place two flowers above the circles. Place the third flower lower than the circles.

Design XII: Line Design With Oriental Influence

LINE DESIGNS: adapted from the Oriental, are those in which the linear pattern is dominant. They are characterized by restraint in the quantity of plant materials used and have an open silhouette.

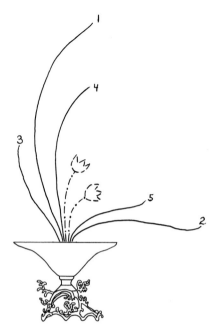

Container
Japanese bronze

Plant Material
5 polygonum branches
2 flowers may be added or
2 more polygonum branches

Mechanics
Pinholder

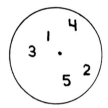

Placement on Pinholder

Procedure

Cut #1 branch to be the tallest and strongest. Place in left back of center on pinholder.

#2 branch shorter than #1. Place low and to the right front.

#3 branch shorter than #2. Place to the left front of #1.

#4 branch shorter than #3. Place to the right back of #1.

#5 branch shorter than #4. Place to the center front over edge of container.

Note: Two flowers or small polygonum branches may be added in the space between #4 and #5. They should be leaning slightly forward.

Substitute Container: Any low container or compote.

Glossary

Abstract Design - a creative design in which plant material and other components are used solely as line, form, color and texture, in space, to create new images.

Asymmetrical Balance - approximate equal visual weight composed of different elements on each side of a vertical axis; balance without symmetry.

Asymmetrical Mass Design - a right triangle characterized by the use of a large quantity of plant material. The plant material is not crowded.

Components - physical material of which a design is composed; plant material, container, any special staging and mechanics.

Conditioning - preparation of cut plant material before arranging.

Container - any receptacle to hold plant material.

Creative Mass - a design using more plant material than other present day designs. There may be enclosed spaces resulting from the placement of line materials and these spaces are considered part of the mass. Groupings of plant materials of like colors, textures and forms are massed along lines, or spaces made by lines. Containers are usually non-traditional. There may be more than one focal area and more than one point of emergence; however, the design is not abstract.

Creative Vertical - the dominant thrust of the design must be vertical. There may be more than one point of emergence and more than one focal area if it does not destroy the vertical thrust.

Design Elements - the basic visual qualities of a design: light, space, line, form, size, color, texture and pattern.

Design Principles - basic standards of art used to organize design elements: balance, proportion, scale, rhythm, dominance and contrast.

Diagonal Design - plant material extends in a slanting line, from one angle to another, not adjacent.

Filler Plant Material - transitional plant material used to fill in between different plant forms.

Fresh Plant Material - any part severed from a living plant, in fresh condition.

Gradation - a sequence in which there is a regular and orderly change in size, form, color or texture.

Grooming - cleaning flowers to remove dirt and spray residue as well as dead or broken foliage or flowers.

Hardening - to place plant material in water several hours before arranging.

Horizontal Design - a design that is always wider than it is tall.

Line Design - a design in which the linear pattern is dominant.

Mass Design - characterized by the use of a large quantity of plant material. The plant material is not crowded, but the design has a closed silhouette, meaning there are no open spaces within the outline of the design.

Mechanics - contrivances used to hold and control materials in design.

Parallel Design - has three or more vertical groupings of materials. Open spaces between the groupings are important.

Pincup - lead cup with needles to hold water and plant material.

Pinholder - needles on a lead base to hold plant material.

Spike Flower - a lengthened flower cluster in which flowers are practically stemless. Examples: gladiolus, snapdragon, liatris.

Symmetrical Balance - similar on two sides of a real or imaginary vertical axis.

Vertical Design - one with a strong upward thrust and with greater height than width.

With appreciation to the National Council of State Garden Clubs, Inc. for permission to use selected definitions from its Handbook For Flower Shows.

Index